MW01170022

木村恵子
Keiko Kimura

ARE THE JAPANESE REALLY INSCRUTABLE?

Keiko Kimura

MINERVA PRESS

LONDON
ATLANTA MONTREUX SYDNEY

ARE THE JAPANESE REALLY INSCRUTABLE
Copyright © Keiko Kimura 1998

All Rights Reserved

No part of this book may be reproduced in any form,
by photocopying or by any electronic or mechanical means,
including information storage or retrieval systems,
without permission in writing from both the copyright
owner and the publisher of this book.

ISBN 0 75410 396 X

First Published 1998 by
MINERVA PRESS
Sixth Floor
Canberra House
315–317 Regent Street
London W1R 7YB

Printed in Great Britain for Minerva Press

ARE THE JAPANESE
REALLY INSCRUTABLE?

Preface

The Japanese are all over the world these days. Those who have ever had contact with us might have found something 'strange,' 'different,' or 'inscrutable' about our behavior. This book has been written to give some clue to why the Japanese behave in this way. It is especially meant for the following:

- Host families accommodating Japanese students in their homes.
- ESL teachers who teach Japanese children in their classrooms.
- Students who study the Japanese language and culture.
- Professors who teach Japanese students.
- Those who have a Japanese family in the neighborhood.
- Students who have Japanese roommates at college.
- Workers who have a Japanese boss or colleague.
- Anyone planning to move to or already living in Japan.
- Staff who work in hotels and shops serving Japanese customers, etc.

Here is an example that illustrates the concept gap between Americans and Japanese. Baseball is one of the most popular sports among the Japanese. As with football in the US and soccer in Europe, many Japanese watch baseball. So far, though, Japan has exported only a few baseball players to the US and there is a trend among Japanese professional baseball teams to employ American players at very high salaries to strengthen their team. A certain player was an American who was well known among baseball fans for his excellent record. However, one year he stopped playing in the middle of the season and returned to the US with his family. His six-year-old son had become seriously ill and needed to be treated in the US. The Japanese baseball team that had employed the player became angry because he had left Japan in the middle of the season and did not return on the date he promised, so they discharged him.

The player, surprised at this sudden discharge, sued the team for the medical costs for his son. Believe it or not, though, he and his family were not covered by medical insurance. According to the contract, the team was to pay all medical expenses in cash in any case as needed. His son was diagnosed with a brain tumor, and you can imagine how expensive medical treatment was in the US, especially for such a serious illness. The discharged player wanted these bills paid by the team. The commissioner of the team had to handle the negotiations between the discharged player and the team. He was an earnest man, and when he realized his efforts had failed, despite all his pains, he threw himself from a hotel window, after saying goodbye to his wife over the phone. This affair, which drove an innocent man to his death, was caused by a lack of understanding between two cultures.

What went wrong?

First, there is a different approach to family in Japan. Americans believe that the family is the first priority, especially if a child is facing death, and many readers of this book would sympathize with the player's decision. Yet things are different for the Japanese. Of course we Japanese love our families as much as the Americans, but our approach is different. The family is identified as one unit, so a Japanese person must meet social responsibilities even if it means a sacrifice to the family. In this case, many Japanese people would have expected the player's wife to take care of the child alone, while her husband played until the end of the season.

Second, the discharged player took the issue to court. This is a very common way of solving problems for Americans. However, for the Japanese, taking issues to court is a final resort. Even with major quarrels, the Japanese will first try to negotiate; we will give and take as much as possible to find a position of compromise. Only when this fails will any issue be taken to court. The Japanese baseball team, then, was surprised to hear that the player had gone to court without attempting any negotiation. The poor commissioner, who was placed between the player and the team, sacrificed his life to show his sincere feelings for both the player and the team. For the Japanese, taking one's own life is done to prove one's innocence.

If this story seems strange or engages your interest, I hope you will read on and gain further clues to understanding Japanese thinking. It is not necessary to read this book in order from beginning to end. You may pick it up at any chapter you are interested in.

Chapter One

Harmony

In Japanese society, the most important aspect of being a good citizen is keeping harmony with others. The people who are regarded as ideal citizens are the ones who live ordinary lives within their means, not those who have radical personalities or exceptional abilities; the ones who keep to the rules of society in all circumstances rather than those who ask questions and try to change tradition are regarded as the more admirable.

This spirit of keeping harmony among people within a group is called *wa* in Japanese. This means that people who always think in terms of harmony with others, perhaps saying, 'I am what you are', would be more respected than someone like Popeye who says, 'I am what I am'.

The origin of the idea of *wa* appears in the constitution of Prince Shotuku in AD 604. It states, 'Have respect for *wa*', and further on, *wa* is explained as the standard to rule the people as a group.

Today when a group seeks a decision in Japan, people prefer negotiation and compromise rather than any type of showdown. If they have different opinions, people try to persuade each other to reach the middle ground. This is why the Japanese believe *wa* is more important than individual intentions, and why the Japanese scarcely express our own (individual) opinions in public, often depending on others when we need to make decisions.

Let me give you a typical example. Suppose a Japanese goes to a restaurant in America, or any other Western country for that matter. The hardest thing for him is to decide what he wants to eat and drink. The menu has a dizzying variety of wines, soups, hors d'oeuvres, salads, dressings, steaks (rare? medium? well-done?), desserts, cheeses, tea or coffee, cream or sugar and so on. Many Japanese people hate to go to Western restaurants because it is simply too much for them to make a dozen or more choices for the sake of a single dinner.

If you go to an authentic Japanese restaurant, your decision-making is much easier. Often times you can see a menu which reads, 'Course A (¥10,000), Course B (¥7,000), Course C (¥5,000), Lunch Special (¥3,000)'. It will only take a minute to make a decision, because it will be determined purely by your budget for that night. If there are things you dislike in a course you choose, you simply leave them uneaten. If your budget is especially large one night, you may even order the *omakase* (chef's choice) special. This leaves the chef free to invent whatever the season inspires. In Japan, decisions are often made by others.

Having different opinions is an inevitable part of a group decision-making process, yet if a simple majority of a group decides to enforce a certain decision in spite of the opposition, there will remain a highly tense atmosphere among both the majority and the opposition. In order to avoid this emotional entanglement, the members of the group strive to reach compromise on the various points of a conflict. As expressed in an ancient Japanese proverb, 'Minor differences must be submerged for greater common interests. Differences in detail should be ignored, and agreement in principles be upheld.' Even if only a few people are discontent, a group will try to reach a compromise so that their decisions or proposals will be adopted unanimously. This is the same logic as the meal at the Japanese restaurant: eat what is good in each course and leave what you dislike uneaten.

In order to obtain unanimous consent, members of a group work hard behind the scenes to examine, revise, and improve a proposal so as to obtain at least unofficial consent before the meeting. Thus, everybody understands and agrees, at least superficially, in the final vote at the official meeting. Such agreement is the unspoken standard among the Japanese, by which people share their likes and dislikes with each other in order to reach a peaceful solution. At the base of this system lies the optimistic view that human nature as a whole is fundamentally good. The Japanese believe that we can understand each other because we are a single race with a single language.

On the other hand, the Japanese do not get along with the law. This is because we believe that the law was created on the basis that man is fundamentally evil, and that if the law did not exist society would degenerate at the hands of evil. Before the Meiji era (1868–1912) an official notice from the authorities was a one-sided order, and a tool of a ruler by which to enslave his people. The people simply obeyed orders and took punishments without question because they did not have any sense of security about their rights, or the laws defending them. After that era, many laws, including those in the newly constructed constitution, were enacted, yet those laws were modeled after Western countries' laws and were never fully adopted by the Japanese culture. This does not mean that the Japanese people's awareness of their rights as citizens was undeveloped. It would, however, indicate that the traditional courtesies, conventions, or morals maintained precedence over the new law. The people, then, preferred solving problems on their own with *wa* rather than depend upon the law.

The verdict in a Japanese court is dependent upon a simple majority voted by judges. However, if an issue is settled legally with a winner and a loser, there remains great tensions between the two parties forever. This is at the heart of the conflict with *wa*.

Even today, both the victims and perpetrators of accidents try to avoid bringing matters to court. Instead, they take time to discuss the dispute through a mediator and find a point where both are able to compromise and solve the problem. The number of civil suits in Japan is one fortieth of that of the civil suits in the US (4,859,000 cases in the US per year and 126,000 in Japan).

In capital crimes, the victim's family would prefer to settle the matter, but if matters get out of hand, they would rather give up arguing knowing that either way their loved one(s) would not return.

Only in the worst cases, where discussion is fruitless, do people bring the case to court. This is supported by an interesting statistic. Japan's proportion of lawyers is one eighteenth of that in America and one eighth that of Great Britain. One in 8,200 people in Japan is a lawyer, while in America the ratio is one in 328.

Chapter Two

Humility

We Japanese have a tendency to disparage ourselves when we talk with others. This means we make ourselves lower and others higher. When the Japanese express their humility, we are often showing our respect for others.

The first time you were invited to a Japanese home, were you surprised when the host invited you to the table saying, 'We have nothing... but...?' Did you think, 'How would you not have anything? You offered an invitation.' And when you got to the table, you found that there was a table overflowing with food. Or when you were given a gift, maybe the person offering it said, 'This is really nothing...', and this 'nothing' happened to be an expensive gift.

A Japanese professor invited to speak to a group in Washington opened his speech by saying, 'Thank you for inviting me today. First I have to apologize that I did not prepare anything for this speech,' in a Japanese way. However, among the predominantly American audience, a murmur spread. 'He knew about this lecture months ago. He should have prepared something,' they were saying. But when the speech began, it was obvious that it had been prepared very carefully from beginning to end. The audience was surprised once again.

In Japan, people who are independent-minded, or who like to show their intelligence or knowledge, are not well-liked. Active, positive, and frank persons are not much liked either. Whatever their age and status, people who are reserved and modest are looked upon as being good and refined and having foresight. Therefore, the Japanese do not take the word of other Japanese people at face value. We know that even when we say, 'We have nothing', it is probably going to be an excellent meal, and that 'this nothing' will probably be a delightful gift. As for the person knowing about the speech for over a month: of course, he will have prepared a very well-thought-out paper. However, if someone were to say, 'We have a delicious meal, so please eat', or, 'We have a wonderful present here', or, 'Because I am an expert in this field and no one else can do better,' the person would not be well-liked. Even a politician's speech will reflect this by saying, 'I am nobody, but I would like to keep studying and serve you.' Even if you have ten of something you should not even mention half of them. The more modest you are, the more you are liked.

To be resigned is also one of the arts of communication. In Japan, when you are offered something, it is expected that to be polite you will refuse the first time. (It is said that you refuse three times in Kyoto!) For example, when his plate is empty, you ask your guest if he would like more. If the guest is Japanese, even though he may want more he will first refuse. However, the host will insist by saying, 'Please have another bite', and then the person follows by saying, 'Okay, just another bite'. However, in other cultures, 'no' is taken at face value, so if you refuse the first time, the host may say 'okay' and not offer it again.

On the other hand, you may have sincerely refused food and drink and been forced to eat or drink more by Japanese hosts. This is also done because it is believed that you are following the 'Japanese politeness', so do not be angry and think, 'Why do they keep offering despite my refusal?' If you really do not want any more, do not touch your food or drink; they will understand that you really do not want any more, and will stop.

You may think this is a very confusing tradition, but something that has been practiced for years is very difficult to change immediately. Therefore, if you are in Japan, you should do as the Japanese do, but when you notice Japanese people abroad following Japanese manners, please advise them that this does not work in your culture.

Chapter Three

Eye Contact

Eye contact is one of the fundamentals of human communication. Westerners may find it strange that many Japanese people find eye contact very difficult. Perhaps you have noticed that the Japanese may turn their eyes away, or even avoid eye contact altogether, during a conversation. Or perhaps you have walked past a Japanese person who quickly turned his eyes away and looked down shyly.

In each of these situations, you might have thought that the person had no interest in you and was not listening to you. You may have considered such behavior untrustworthy. However, for the Japanese, avoiding eye contact is an established rule of etiquette.

In the US, a teacher who scolds a student may say, 'Listen to me carefully! Look at me when I am talking to you.' However, in Japan, if a student were to look the teacher directly in the eye, it would mean that the student was making a challenge. There, when students are disciplined by a teacher, they do not look at the teacher's face. Rather, they bow their heads and look down at the floor.

A book on Japanese etiquette has this to say about eye contact:

When you are listening to a person intently, the eye should be focused within a square formed by the space between the speaker's eyes, chest and shoulders.

When you are listening to a person casually, the eye should be focused within a square formed by the space between the forehead, bellybutton and shoulders.

Even current business magazines have advised people preparing for job interviews to look at the top of the interviewer's tie. When in a business meeting, the magazine further advises looking at the top of the other person's nose. To look straight into another person's eyes creates tension; therefore, it is agreed that you should look directly at a person only when you want to stress a point.

From the time we Japanese are young, we are taught that to look into a person's eyes is to look into that person's heart, and is an aggressive act. Therefore, avoiding eye contact is especially important for Japanese women. Eye contact is used to categorize human relationships in Japan. For example, a person above you in society is called 'above eye', while a person of lower status is called 'below eye'. This hierarchy was established when Japan was a warrior society in which a shogun, seated above the rest, looked down on his subjects. Even now, it is considered rude to look down at your superiors. For example, if you are descending the stairs and notice that a superior is climbing up the stairs, you should pretend not to notice until you reach the same level. This is when you exchange your greetings.

In Japanese homes, the entrance is a step up from the door. Therefore, in order not to appear rude by looking down at a guest, it is proper to kneel to welcome the guest.

In an office, it is customary to bow to each other. A bow is a traditional way of greeting people in Japan. Since both heads come down at the same time, eye contact is naturally avoided. No one can look directly at the other person while bowing. It is impolite to look directly at people whom you do not know well. When children are young, mother and child often communicate by looking at each other, but as the child grows older, eye contact decreases.

In Japan, you will notice that people tend to read or sleep on the bus or train. This may be because they want to read a book or because they are sleepy, but many do it to avoid eye contact. In the US, if you accidentally make eye contact, smiles are usually exchanged. However, in Japan, it creates an uncomfortable atmosphere, and people may quickly look the other way. Therefore, people read or lightly close their eyes.

The first gynecology appointment I had in the US was very shocking. After being told to take off my clothes (I did have a paper covering on me), I had to meet the doctor face to face. Though this is normal practice in the US, in Japan a curtain is drawn across the middle of the bed where you lay down, so you do not see the doctor on the other side of the curtain.

Many ways to avoid eye contact have been woven into Japanese daily life. In a beauty parlor, when you get your hair washed, gauze is placed over your eyes so that eye contact can easily be avoided. In a traditional Japanese home, there is a special space called *tokonoma*, to place flower arrangements or to hang paintings. The host sits in front of this space when welcoming guests; the guest does not need to look at the host directly, but can look at the flowers or paintings.

The Japanese feel most comfortable sitting next to each other on a bench or at a sushi bar facing the same direction. If you watch Japanese movies carefully, lovers often do not face each other, but sit side by side and look toward the river or the moon.

So please remember that when the Japanese avoid eye contact it does not mean that we are ignoring you, or are uninterested in what you are saying. Rather, we are following a Japanese custom.

Chapter Four

Yes and No

Those of you who have spoken to Japanese people have probably noticed that they said, 'yes, yes yes,' as you were talking, and so you thought they were in agreement with you. You may have been surprised to find out later that they were not agreeing with you.

In this case, 'yes' means not that, 'I agree with you', but rather that, 'I understand what you are saying', or, 'I'm following your conversation'. Those who do business with the Japanese especially need to be aware that in Japanese *hai*, does not necessarily equate to your 'yes'.

The Japanese sometimes say 'yes' or give you an affirmative answer instead of saying 'no'.

For the Japanese, it is impolite to express opinions directly, and we have methods of avoiding direct statements. 'No' is rarely used in Japanese expressions. This does not mean that the Japanese have not developed individualism, but that we are trying to avoid unnecessary frictions; avoiding 'no' shows their respect or saves face.

In business meetings or negotiations, the Japanese may end by saying, 'We will look into this further', or, 'We will consider this seriously', or, 'We will reply as soon as possible'. Thinking that you have succeeded in convincing them, you might be disappointed later to find that the answer is not positive. However, if you understood the Japanese at all, you would have known at the time that in such situations there is a 90% chance that the answer will be 'no'.

Another 'yes' and 'no' problem between English-speaking people and the Japanese is caused by grammatical differences between the languages.

If an English-speaking person asks a Japanese person, 'Will you come to the party?', the answer will be, 'Yes, I will' or, 'No, I won't.' This is a normal question and answer and presents no difficulty. The problem will occur if you ask using a negative sentence, such as, 'You won't come to the party, will you?' or 'Don't you like hamburgers?' The Japanese answer will be, 'Yes, I won't come to the party,' and, 'Yes, I don't like hamburgers,' or, 'No, I will come to the party,' or, 'No, I do like hamburgers.'

In the Japanese language, 'yes' and 'no' answers are given according to what you are asked. So when the Japanese answer 'yes' it means, 'Yes you are right' ('I won't go to the party') or, 'No, you are wrong' ('I do like hamburgers'). How confusing!

It is important to understand that for those who have grown up with such grammatical structures, learning English is very confusing. It is important for English speaking people not to judge immediately after hearing a Japanese person say 'yes' or 'no', but to listen carefully to the words following. If you say, 'Don't you understand me?' the answer may be, 'No, I understand you very clearly.'

Chapter Five

Ranking

Japanese people exchange name cards when we meet for the first time. As we catch a glimpse of the card, carefully take a look at one particular point, and start to greet each other. Usually, workplace and title are printed on a name card beside the name. Japanese people read the title carefully before anything else, and instantly we find out our relative positions. If the other is of lower rank, a Japanese person does not need to bow so deeply, and can speak in a familiar tone. If your companion has a higher rank, you need to bow deeply and use honorific expressions when you speak.

Many foreigners who start to study Japanese stumble on these honorific expressions, because you need to choose words according to the rank of the person with whom you are speaking. For example, in English, 'you' is always 'you' to any person, regardless of age, sex, or the relationship between you. But, in Japanese, the expression of 'you' (*anata*) can change to *anta*, *omae*, *otaku*, *kimi*, etc. depending on whether the person you speak with is he or she, old or young, intimate or a stranger, and in higher or lower position to you.

Because the English-Japanese dictionary translates 'you' as *anta*, many foreigners use it. Generally speaking, however, the Japanese rarely use the word *anta* to anyone, especially to superiors or seniors. If you say *anta* to your teacher or boss, they will become angry because they will think you are looking down on them. The word *anta* itself is not an impolite word, but in fact rather polite. Still, Japanese people would never use it to superiors, though we would use it to a subordinate.

When you need to address a superior, you usually use a title like *sensei* (for a professor, teacher, doctor, member of the Japanese Diet, superior), *bucho* (head of division) or *senpai* (senior) instead of *anta*. When you do not use a title, *-san* is used after the surname, as in 'Kimura-*san*'. Instead of *anta*, using the name with *-san* shows respect to the person with whom you are speaking.

The same applies to 'I'. The expression 'I' changes into *watakushi* (for men and women, formal), *boku* (for men and boys, casual), *shohsei* (for men, written), *ore* (for men and boys, coarse), *wagahai* (for men, old-fashioned), and so on, according to whom you are speaking. In the Japanese language, these different personal pronouns may express various feelings or evaluations, such as respect, contempt, or intimacy.

Not only pronouns, but verbs and adverbs also change according to age, sex and ranking. For example, if you read a short English sentence like 'Where are you going?' you don't know the relationship between the speakers. In Japanese, every pronoun, verb, and adverb can be varied, which could make at least ten different sentences depending upon who is speaking to whom. So even if you read a short sentence like 'Where are you going?' in Japanese you will know the relationship between those concerned – man or woman, old person or youth, employee or employer, teacher or student, wife or husband, parent or child.

This relationship by ranking distinguishes not only adults but even children in the Japanese community. For example, in high school, if you are a freshman and talk to a senior, you need to use honorifics. Not only in language, but also in daily life, seniors always have priority.

As in the old Japanese saying, 'yield to the power', many Japanese people follow orders without complaint. You may not say 'no' if your boss invites you to go to a bar after work, even if you wish to go home right away. While drinking, the boss may bring up an important discussion of your work. In Japan, 'after five' is also considered part of the work day.

The majority of new recruits start work planning to stay with that company their whole life. The corporation takes care of the employees as if they are members of a big family, providing housing and vacation resorts at the beach and in the mountains. Some companies provide day care centers for working mothers. To help in marriage, childbirth, or funerals of their employees and their families, the company provides both financial and emotional support. The boss is deeply involved not only in his employees' work, but also in their private lives. He may ask about family troubles, marriage, or even try to play matchmaker.

In a recent survey, Japanese businessmen were asked their opinions of two bosses, A and B. Boss A never asked for unreasonable work or got angry with his employees. He tried to avoid socializing with employees outside work. Boss B was always very demanding at work and often got angry. He was heavily involved in the employees' private lives and took care of them well. If you could choose a boss, asked the survey, which would you choose, A or B? Eighty percent of Japanese businessmen preferred B as their boss. In Japanese society, there is an unspoken rule respecting rank and the relationship between boss and employees which extends into private life.

This relationship is also reflected in family life. The rank of the husband affects his wife. It is very common that the wife of a boss will treat an employee's wife as her subordinate.

Many Japanese corporations provide housing for their employees. Though the rent is low and the location excellent, many employees prefer to live in a private house because their ranking at the company is reflected in their private life, and this makes for more complex human relationships in their social life, especially in an apartment complex.

Chapter Six

Space

The value of physical space varies in different cultures. In Japan, when two people face each other to talk, they must have enough space to greet each other and bow. For Westerners who shake hands and hug, the space needed by the Japanese seems too much. Therefore, when Westerners speak with the people, they move closer to adjust the space, whereupon that Japanese may feel suffocated by the closeness and step backward.

We Japanese like to keep our distance, and there is rarely any physical contact in daily life. We do not hug or kiss – this is true even between husband and wife, and parents and children. Even mothers who hug and kiss their babies only hold hands with their children by the time they enter kindergarten.

My family has lived in the US for over fifteen years, and we have absorbed many American customs. We are able to kiss and hug our close American friends. However, within the family, we maintain the Japanese 'space'. For some Americans, this 'space' seems cold, and friends worry about the relationships within the family, but the five of us are living closely together. We do not need hugs and kisses to know we care for each other.

It is rather ironic that the Japanese have no problems with coming in physical contact with strangers. Those who have traveled by train or bus during rush hour in Japan have experienced the sardine-packed commuter cars. People are crushed against one another in this small space and yet commute to work without complaint. However, when people subsequently find acquaintances next to them in other contexts, they attempt to create space. It is very inconsistent that you can be packed next to strangers, but not to acquaintances.

Many people notice that Japanese tourists do not say 'excuse me' or 'sorry' when they bump into a person on the street. For the Japanese, it is normal to run into people and if we were to apologize every time it happened, we would be apologizing all day long, and would never be able to get to our destinations.

Japanese homes are often described by Westerners as rabbit hutches. Compared with houses in the US, they are definitely smaller. For example, in the US there is an average of 60.9 m^2 floor space per person, in the United Kingdom 35 m^2 per person, and in Japan 25 m^2 floor space per person. However, this small space is not a great concern to the Japanese as others might believe.

This last fact stems from the value of space. The most comfortable space for the Japanese family is the space of 4.5 traditional Japanese *tatami* mats – about nine square feet. In this small space, the family places a small, low, heated table, *kotatsu*, with a coverlet during winter. The family eats, studies, and reads in this little room. There are living rooms that are eight or even ten *tatami* in area, but the family feels most comfortable in the traditional family room. The space allotted in the small room is perfect for a close-knit family. Some Japanese people living in a large house with central heating in the US even bring the *kotatsu* from Japan, place it in the smallest room in the house, and gather together there, because to the Japanese it is the most cozy and comfortably-sized room.

Chapter Seven

Privacy

Traditionally, Japanese houses are made of wood and paper. In contrast, the wall in a house in Germany is two bricks thick (49 cm) and the wall of a townhouse is over 70 cm thick. In Japan, the wall is at most 15 cm thick. On the average, it is 6 cm thick and in some places may only measure 4 cm. As the Japanese say, 'the walls have ears and the *shoji* have eyes', meaning that if you put your ears next to the wall, you could clearly hear the conversation on the other side, and if you wet your finger and made a small hole through the paper in the shoji screen (a sliding door made of white rice paper), you would see what was going on in the next room. Even though you may not be able to see across the entire house, you would be able to hear everything.

In recent years, apartments and apartment complexes, called *danchi* or *manshon*, built of cement and concrete, have increased. However, even inside these modern buildings, rooms with *tatami* are still popular. These matted rooms are separated by *fusuma*, partitions made of hard paper. *Fusuma* can be taken down easily and the large room used as a gathering room. Of course, there are no keys, and partitions can be moved without any effort. Even though the family may be all around the house they can sense each other's presence. This is the nature of privacy in Japan. Westerners may find such close quarters uncomfortable, but this is the type of privacy with which the Japanese are most comfortable.

If you have visited a Japanese company or government office, you may have noticed that very few people have private rooms. Generally, only the president or chief executive officer has a private office. People work side by side in a large room. In a school, there is a room called the teachers' room where all teachers have desks side by side. Even though their work may be completely different, the Japanese find comfort in knowing what the person next to them is doing. Therefore, Japanese people who are sent abroad to work in a different environment are uncomfortable when they are placed in their own offices, not knowing what others are doing. To be in a room with a lock can be frightening, perhaps even terrifying, for a person who has grown up as part of a group, not needing individual space.

In a Japanese house, there is space between the door and the step up to the entrance of the house, called the *genkan*. This entrance space is used to take off shoes when entering the house and putting them back on when leaving. Since the Meiji era, the Japanese have imitated Westerners in clothing and furniture; however, we still have not adjusted to keeping our shoes on. Therefore, this space is still used to store shoes. In addition, it is used for the exchange of greetings between visitor and resident.

The *engawa* is a wooden floor that extends out from the house. Friends may choose not to enter the house, but rather sit and talk on the *engawa*. In Japan, it is quite normal for someone to 'pop in' for a visit. As a matter of fact, to announce your visit may trouble the host to prepare for you. Therefore, it might be said that simply to 'pop in' is actually more considerate of the host. 'Please excuse me at the entrance' is a greeting often used to indicate to the host that you will not be entering the house, but will finish the business at the *genkan* and leave. Since the *genkan* is regarded as a public place, houses in Japan often do not have keys or doorbells, and people open the door and call out '*gomenkudasai*' ('hello'). The *genkan* also means that even door-to-door salespeople can enter the house.

In this way, it can be said that the Japanese do not place a great emphasis on privacy. With the precondition that we are all Japanese and think and do similar things, we find comfort in knowing that others are nearby.

Chapter Eight

Guess

kantan aiterasu (we agree in our innermost thoughts)
ishin-denshin (we understand each other without the
medium of language)

In Japan, there are many proverbs that express how you do
not have to say anything for the other person to understand. For the Japanese, silence is much more valuable than
words.

For example, when a boss is looking for something in
his pocket, a good employee understands immediately that
the boss is looking for cigarettes, and pulls out his own box
and hands it to the boss (a person rummaging in his coat
pocket is clearly looking for cigarettes). When the same
person taps a cigarette on the table, the employee can guess
that the boss is about to smoke, and offers his own lighter.
When the cigarette is lit, the employee rushes to fetch an
ashtray to place in front of the boss. During this time, the
boss and the employee may never exchange a word. The
employee takes the smallest hints from the boss and
presumes or understands the next step. The boss is likely to
think well of the employee for this.

An example of one of the many things that Japanese
people living in the US find difficult is to be invited for tea
and to be asked, 'Would you like tea or coffee?' In Japan,
drinks and sweets are prepared with the season or the guest

in mind. Therefore, in the hot summer, iced tea may be ready, and during the cold winter, hot green tea may be prepared. The host normally serves these drinks without consulting the guest, who gracefully accepts the prepared drink. If you can't take it for some reason, it is quite acceptable not to drink it.

In Western cultures, old friends and new acquaintances can meet and talk easily among themselves at tea gatherings. On the other hand, a traditional Japanese tea party is performed in silence while guests listen to the stream flowing through the garden or the bamboo handle of a ladle hitting against the water pot. They quietly enjoy the tea prepared by the host, while looking at the paintings and other crafts in the room. The host and the guests may exchange a short greeting, but as the guests are sitting on the floor, lined up in front of the host, they do not exchange words with each other. In this atmosphere, the people in the whole room are opening their hearts and communicating in silence. This atmosphere is similar to the image of the famous stone garden in Kyoto called Ryouanji where there are no trees or plants in the garden, just white pebbles and large rocks arranged to create a quiet peaceful place.

Communication for the Japanese, therefore, is often silent. Thoughts do not need words to be expressed. When Japanese people become close to one another, it is said that words need not be used. Therefore, if a husband and wife appear not to be talking with each other, it does not mean they are not communicating.

As noted in my chapter on privacy, the *fusuma* (heavy paper partitions) that separate traditional Japanese rooms do not insulate the room very well. It can easily be broken. However, the meaning of this word is, 'barrier'. There is an understanding that you do not listen to what you hear across the *fusuma*. If the *fusuma* is closed, you have to guess whether the person in the other room will welcome you or not. Without this kind of custom, group living among the Japanese would never be successful.

For thousands of years, Japan has never been invaded by another country. Therefore, a homogeneous group with one language prevails in Japan. It is fundamentally believed that whether it is the person next door or a person thousands of miles away, if they are Japanese, they will understand each other. And the thought follows that if they can communicate without speaking, then words are unnecessary. Therefore, chatterers have long been looked down upon, while those who choose not to speak are revered.

This was a great influence on the development of the Japanese language. Japanese sentences often do not use subjects or objects, but only verbs. For example, 'Go?' instead of saying 'Do you go to school?' This would be in a normal conversation, where, depending on the situation, you would understand the context without being told. When 'I love you' in English is translated directly into Japanese, it becomes '*watashiwa (boku) anatao aishimasu.*' However, this is strictly computer or robot language and would sound strange to a Japanese person. If you were to say that to your Japanese lover, he or she would probably laugh. You just need to look into his eyes or hold her hand.

When translating Japanese into English, it is very difficult to fix on the subject of the sentence. In a Japanese sentence, it can easily be interpreted several ways. This kind of 'space' actually lets the reader imagine and use the mind more. Some writers even say that the job of the writer is not to describe everything, but rather to bring out the reader's imagination. However, when such sentences are translated into English, they often lose this ambiguity.

Therefore it is sometimes easier to read and understand books which have been translated into English. However, to a Japanese reader, the story may be too simple. Furthermore, for many Japanese people, reading sentences that describe everything is quite boring.

Chapter Nine

Love vs. Duty

It is very hard to translate into English two particular words which are quite common among the Japanese, *giri* and *ninjo*. In a rough translation, *ninjo* means love, humaneness, sympathy, warm heartedness, kindness, tenderness, human nature, and common sense while *giri* means a sense of duty, obligation, a debt of gratitude, a sense of honor, responsibility, social courtesy, demand of custom, for the sake of justice, for decency's sake. In short, *giri* is an action or behavior in which you pretend to have *ninjo*, even if there is no sense of it.

In her book The *Chrysanthemum and the Sword*, Ruth Benedict comments on *giri*: 'There is no possible English equivalent, and of all the strange categories of moral obligation which anthropologists find in the cultures of the world, it is one of the most curious.' But is this true? People can find this kind of *modus vivendi* in every culture.

Suppose you and your spouse, having made no other plans, decide to go to a fancy restaurant and a movie afterward on a Saturday evening, but later receive an invitation for a party on that day from your boss. You do not like the boss at all, but you cannot ignore the invitation because it is quite important for your work, so you give up both restaurant and movie and go to the party. You pretend that you are enjoying the party to make the host happy.

In another case, the doorbell rings. When you open the door you find a girl from your neighborhood selling cookies for fund-raising for her school program. You do not need the cookies, but you decide to buy one because her parents are friends of yours and the cookies are not expensive.

When you go to a restaurant, you may leave a tip even if you did not receive good enough service from the waiter, because this is a custom of your society.

All these actions represent *giri*. *Giri* are deeds done against your real feelings to save face, avoid blame by others or avoid social punishment.

However, *giri* does not mean the same as duty in Western society. Duty has a binding power which has nothing to do with people and human feelings, whereas *giri* is seen as pertaining more to personal and emotional human relations. Usually, people do not need to apply *giri* among intimate human relations such as between husband and wife, parent and child, lovers, and so on. It comes about when people feel the need to return the kindness which is shown by people who belong to the same social community. Showing or not showing *giri* to the people who belong to the same social community becomes an indicator of whether one is regarded as a member of that community.

The basic condition for *giri* in a given situation is that both people are members of the same society. Once this is established, this human relationship continues for a long time. Therefore, if you are a foreigner and living in Japan, nobody will complain that you do not show *giri*, because you are not considered a member of the Japanese community.

However, if you are married to a Japanese person and live within Japanese society, you may feel some pressure to follow Japanese customs. Yet the Japanese are very tolerant people (or perhaps very exclusive). They do not care whether you follow Japanese traditions because many Japanese people believe that only they can understand Japanese thought: it cannot be helped that you do not understand a Japanese custom, because you are not Japanese.

The Japanese saying, 'to be torn between *ninjo* (love) and *giri* (duty)' describes the mental suffering caused by conflict between desire coming from one's own heart, and social duty.

For example, a father may want to stay home and play with his children on a Sunday, but he needs to go play golf with his clients. Or you give a gift to your boss even if you do not respect your boss at all. Going to play golf with his clients may bring a person more business and will make a profit for the company, and giving a gift to the boss may facilitate a promotion and provide a smoother relationship in the office.

Thus, *giri* helps smooth over human relationships, much like lubricating oil, and has priority over *ninjo* in Japanese society.

If an emergency meeting was announced at my husband's office on our wedding anniversary on which we had planned to go to a fancy restaurant, my husband would probably think, 'The restaurant will be open tomorrow, but this meeting is only held today.' He would postpone our anniversary dinner to attend the meeting. Of course, like a good Japanese wife, I would let him go without any argument. Like other generous wives, I would send him off with a smile.

Though at times it seems as if the commercial Western civilization has penetrated the young Japanese generation, who seem to live freely without being bound by traditions, many of them still follow these old social rules. For example, people have started to celebrate St Valentine's

Day in Japan. It is quite strange, but the Japanese St Valentine's Day has evolved into a day on which women give chocolate to the men they love. Generally speaking, since women are passive in many ways in Japanese society, this is the only day a woman can express her love to a man. But, if girls and women give chocolate only to their loves, other boys and men around them would feel left out. So it has become a habit that women give smaller chocolates to men who are classmates or colleagues of the men they love. Because these smaller chocolates are given to men out of 'giri', not as a sign of true love, they are called *giri chocho* in Japanese. These *giri chocho* have now created a very good market for chocolate; I would say that the Japanese chocolate industry could be supported by *giri*.

Chapter Ten

Grouping

If you go to Japan, you will find many men wear badges on their lapels. These badges are symbols of the company to which they belong. You will also find that school children in Japan wear school uniforms. Since every school has a different uniform, people can recognize which school a child attends by the uniform. Even in schools with no uniforms, which are rare, students are required to wear a school badge. The Japanese have a desire to show publicly the place where we belong. We are very conscious of that place.

It can be said that the Japanese feel more comfortable with a group than alone. It is also true that, on this basis, we change our attitude toward people whether we know them well or not, that is, we judge a person based on whether he or she is an insider or an outsider.

In Japanese society, relationships as an insider or an outsider are not static but dynamic. It is comparable with the difference between chess and *shogi* (Japanese chess). In chess, your chessmen are always yours even if you lose the pieces. It means the white team is always white and the black team is always black and they never change color. But, in Japanese *shogi*, if you lose a piece, it becomes your opponent's. For example, a pawn becomes your opponent's piece to play when you lose it; a chessman that was on your side suddenly changes to become your enemy. Human relationships in Japan are similar to *shogi*. A person will be an insider or an outsider depending upon the situation.

For example, if you think of your family as a closed unit, your neighbor becomes an outsider. But then the Japanese see all Japanese people as insiders when confronted with foreigners – outsiders. Many Japanese people say, 'We Japanese', when we talk about Japan to foreigners. The concept of insider and outsider will change according to the situation.

Human relations can be divided into three categories.

The first category is the relationships which are very close to you. You know each other very well and there is little reservation between you.

The second category is the relationships which bind you in some other sense, such as with colleagues or classmates. In this category, you must have certain reservations, and you have to think about *giri* in these relationships.

The third category is the relationships in which you have no intimate connection, as with total strangers. In this category, no reservations or *giri* affect you.

The relationships between wife and husband and parents and children are of the first category. In this relationship, people often identify the members of the group as being at one. Because they are at one, a wife does not have to put on make-up or a dress for her husband. They never oppose each other's opinions in public because they have a deep alliance with each other.

The second category includes the relationships with colleagues, classmates, neighbors, friends – anyone who has something to do with your daily life. In these relationships, certain reservations, modesty, and *giri* toward one another are very important. In this category, the definitions of outsider and insider may change according to different situations. I will give you a good example. When my husband and I went to a newly opened Japanese restaurant in Washington, the establishment was having trouble with the electricity in the kitchen. The customers, who were getting irritated because of the long wait, were all Americans except us. When a Japanese waitress recognized us, she came to our table, gave a sigh of relief and said, 'We really are in trouble. I cannot believe this happened on our opening day...' She started to speak of her troubles in Japanese as if we were close friends, although we had never met before. The reason she confided in us was obviously because she regarded us as insiders since we were also Japanese. Since we were customers like the Americans, we expected to hear a word of apology from her. However, instead of giving us this, she complained about her troubles in Japanese and got rid of her stress.

In June 1972, a young Japanese terrorist known as a member of the PLO fired his rifle at random into a group of Jewish passengers at Tel Aviv airport and caused many casualties. The Japanese government immediately decided to present the Israeli government with 460 million Yen (about one and a half million US dollars) as a mark of sympathy. This is because the Japanese believe that a crime committed by one Japanese person is a crime committed by all the Japanese. The young Japanese man was not a government employee. The only reason money was given was because he was a Japanese citizen: if one insider commits a crime, it is believed that all members of the group have an obligation to make restitution to the victims.

In relationships in the third category, it is not necessary to win the good opinion of the other members, or pay attention to them, because they are complete strangers. The people who belong to this group are always regarded as outsiders.

Sometimes, Japanese tourists abroad behave rudely, and are frowned on by foreigners. As an old Japanese proverb says, '*tabino hajiwa kakisute* (a man away from home need feel no shame)', or, 'a traveler is free to be loose in morals.' Many Japanese people think that the people they meet during their travels are strangers whom they will never see again; therefore it is not necessary to think of *giri* or discretion.

For the same reason people are pushy in a crowded commuter train or litter papers and cans on the street or pick flowers from a public park, because people on trains are all outsiders and streets and parks are not your or your friends' yard. Unfortunately, in Japan there is little sense of 'public morality' as there is in Western cultures.

Chapter Eleven

System

In any society, people create systems. Sometimes these systems are created only in the imagination, and will not fit into real life. In Japan, official agreements or systems are called *tatemae* and people's real intentions are called *honne*.

Since the Japanese are a homogeneous nation, it is believed that there are universal and absolute standards among us which apply to everyone, all the time, everywhere. In short, the premise that everybody thinks the same way makes for *tatemae*.

The Japanese people make appropriate use of *tatemae* and *honne* according to different situations. Usually they apply *tatemae* as a shield to judge outsiders, reserving *honne* for insiders.

During World War II, when one mother was seeing her drafted son off to war at a train station, she shouted, '*Banzai*! It is the highest honor to die for the Emperor.' Yet it is obvious that no mother is willing to send her son to the battlefield, and this one must have broken down when she was alone. Soldiers also went to die saying, 'Long live the Emperor!' yet few believed that this was the true voice of a young man willingly giving up his life at such a young age. Some must have anguished over their fate, asking, 'Why was I born at this time?' or, 'Why should I die for the Emperor?' or, 'Why should I die leaving my loved ones behind?' as *honne*. Yet it was an unspoken rule in Japanese society to say, 'Long live the Emperor!' in public at that time, as *tatemae*.

In Japanese society, people talk *tatemae* in public and *honne* in private. *Tatemae* always has priority over *honne*.

Even in law, the Japanese are allowed two faces, to obey officially and to disobey unofficially.

You might be surprised, for example, to hear that Japan has a law against abortion, because Japan is regarded as one of the most 'loose' countries for abortions. As *tatemae*, the law clearly prohibits abortions (Criminal Law Articles 212–16). Yet many women need to have abortions out of *honne*, so there is a loophole called the 'Eugenic Protection Act'. According to this act, it is legal to have an abortion when a woman shows there are any physical, economic, or emotional reasons why a pregnancy would injure or hurt her.

Japan has an anti-prostitution law as *tatemae*. Since this was established in 1955, official red-light districts have died out. Yet, prostitution thrives all over Japan; the businesses have simply changed their names to such things as 'Turkish Bath' or 'Soap Land.' Within *honne*, some people need such places, and the police turn a blind eye to them.

Pornography is also prohibited by Criminal Law Article 175. Obscenity is defined as the showing of pubic hair in art, photographs, or films. Therefore, anything is allowed as long as pubic hair is not shown. You will see many pornographic pictures in Japan, not only in pornography magazines but also in general weekly magazines produced by famous publishers. Comics and cartoons are read by both adults and children, and are very popular. There are a lot of 'semi-' pornographic comics everywhere, even in children's books. People open and read such magazines in public places like commuter trains without any sense of shame these days. In spite of being prohibited by law, many

Japanese people are so accustomed to seeing pornography that it could be called 'chronic pornographic syndrome'.

This is typical of the Japanese society that creates laws to prohibit an activity out of *tatemae*, yet within *honne* allows it secretly or even openly, and tries to ignore it.

This ambiguous Japanese ethic which uses *tatemae* and *honne* according to the situation might preserve a conflict-free life in Japan, in contrast to the failure of the alcohol prohibition law in the US where they didn't listen to people's *'honne'*, of wanting to drink and made the law too strict and without loopholes.

Chapter Twelve

Contract

For the Japanese, a contract is just a piece of paper. A human relationship that depends on a contract of written promises makes one feel that the relationship is lacking intimacy. To make a contract on the assumption that your partner may break his or her part of it means that you do not trust each other. There is a philosophy among the Japanese that you can negotiate when problems occur.

For example, it is neither necessary nor expected to sign a contract with publishers. It makes no difference to have a written contract in Japanese society, and, indeed, it is considered a waste of time and labor. Of course, there will be some cases in which contracts are made, but usually it is only a formality and does not carry much meaning. If you look at a ready-made contract drawn up in Japan which is a standard contract for two parties in which most of the agreements are already written out, you may find a sentence that reads, 'If you find a conflict between the contractors about the contract, try to solve it by discussing the problem with each other,' or, 'Make an agreement by discussion'. If so, why do they need to make a contract?

Suppose someone wants to rent a house. Usually, the owner and the tenant exchange a contract about the fees and the terms. However, in many cases, this is not binding. Since the law protects the rights of the tenant, the tenant may sometimes stay after the term is over. There was one court case in Tokyo between the owner of a high-rise building and a tenant. The owner of the building wanted to renovate his building and therefore did not renew but terminated the leasing contract with the tenants. A tenant who was making a good profit in his shop in this building did not agree with the termination of the contract, and sued the owner. The tenant won the case.

For the Japanese, it is hard to believe that written provisions bind people's lives and have authority beyond the human mind. Japanese people would never demand an inhumane thing on the basis of a contract, like Shylock in the 'Merchant of Venice'. This is again because the Japanese believe that all people think the same way since they are one race, one language, and one culture.

The general understanding for the Japanese people is that 'We are all the same people, so why do we need to prepare for issues which have not occurred? Let's talk to each other when it happens.' This view works fine in Japan. However, the Japanese view on contracts has become a serious problem since Japan began trading with other countries.

Suppose a Japanese company purchased a ten million-dollar precision machine from a manufacturer in country A, but the machine broke down after a year. As soon as the Japanese company reported the trouble to the manufacturer, a mechanical engineer would be sent and would fix it immediately. The Japanese company would think the service was under warranty, yet would receive a bill for the repair, as well as for the airfare for the engineer. The Japanese company would ask about the warranty, and might be told, 'The warranty of this machine lasts one year. The machine broke down five days after the date of the warranty. Therefore you have a responsibility for the payment.'

Many Japanese would think that if this happened with a Japanese machine, the manufacturer would be embarrassed about the problem and would repair it at no cost, or at least would give a discount rate. Therefore, an attitude like that of the manufacturer in country A, refusing service because the breakdown occurred five days after the warranty expired, would be considered cold and incomprehensible by the Japanese. And there would be no words of apology from the manufacturer.

In Japan, if you apologize, all will be forgiven. When a big accident happens, the person responsible will make a statement of apology with a very deep bow in front of the family of the victims. Then they will start to negotiate the compensation. To make an apology means that you take responsibility for the problem. This is why such negotiations run quite smoothly.

Western people say, 'I'm sorry' or, 'Excuse me' quite often for very small things, like touching somebody by mistake while walking on a crowded street. Yet they never say a word of apology for a big accident, because they are afraid of being blamed for it. The first thing they have to do is to solve the problem (pay money to the victim) according to the agreement of the contract.

In Japan, people prefer sincerity to money. For example, visiting victims at the hospital or attending a funeral service will have a lot of impact on people. On the contrary, if you hire a lawyer for the negotiations, this can create tension between the victims and the negotiators.

As for the American baseball player mentioned at the beginning, if he had apologized at first for his actions and then explained how serious his son's illness was, begging for forgiveness with tears, matters might have ended in a different way.

Chapter Thirteen

Sticking Nail

Deru kuiwa utareru is a Japanese proverb which means, 'The nail that sticks out will be hammered down.' This means that if you are different from others or conspicuous in society, you will be isolated and kept away from the rest.

There are many examples, but let us focus on of students returning from overseas.

Japan's post-war economic progress has caused more and more Japanese businessmen to work outside Japan, and there are an increasing number of Japanese families who live overseas. The parents have a firm Japanese identity; therefore they seldom have an identity crisis living abroad. However, their children easily accept a different culture as their own. They learn and adopt different value systems, speak the native language without any accent, and behave as their friends do. The parents start to worry about their children and try to keep up their Japanese identity, forcing them to go to Japanese school at weekends or use Japanese books and videos. Yet the speed with which the children absorb foreign cultures is much faster than their parents may imagine.

Children do well in local schools, make good friends, and adjust to the culture very well. However, they cannot stay there forever. Once the father is ordered to return home, the family must follow him. For the parents, it is exciting to be going home because Japan is their homeland

and they look forward to seeing relatives and friends. Yet for the children who spent several years in a foreign country, Japan is no longer their home. They are pure Japanese genetically, but not mentally. In Japan, they often have to go to school with the same uniforms, the shoes, the school bags, and hairstyles. Many returning students are ill-suited to the conformity of Japanese culture, not only in appearance, but also in ways of thinking.

For students returning from English-speaking countries, English classes are torture. If the English teacher were a broad-minded person, he or she could use the returning student as an assistant, and the whole class could benefit.

Unfortunately, many English teachers who have never been overseas, avoid or are annoyed by the returning student who sometimes knows English better than the teacher. When the student reads English sentence with a real accent, the rest of the class may start to giggle because the pronunciation is so much different from what they have learned. If the teacher were brave enough to say that his or her pronunciation was wrong and the returning student's was right, the class would understand it. But many narrow-minded teachers who are afraid of losing their authority will say, 'We never learn such a coarse New York English accent in the classroom; we study authentic Queen's English.'

If the returning student points out some sentence which would never be used, the teacher may say, 'This may not be used in New York, but remember that it will be seen on the entrance examination for college in Japan.'

It would be better if there could be discussions between the teachers and the returning students, even if they are bitter ones. But many teachers avoid such students and pretend that they do not exist in the classroom. The returning students gradually come to understand the situation, and some become more acquiescent in their character. If they are asked to read an English sentence in the classroom they purposely try to read with a Japanese accent and they do not open their mouths even if the teacher is wrong. In order to maintain a good relationship with their classmates, they hide their overseas experience and try to be the same as the other students as much as possible.

A positive attitude, respect for individuality, a broad vision, the spirit of criticism – all are important elements for living in a complex international society. These are values that children learn by living in different cultures, and are destroyed by Japanese society.

It is not only returning students, but also those regular Japanese students who are a little bit different from others, who are left out as well. For example, most Japanese have straight, black hair. However, there are some people who have a natural wave in their hair or a little bit of red. Yet many schools have rules which prohibit hair which is permed or dyed; those who have a natural curl or red hair by birth are sometimes required to present their 'natural curl certificates'(!) or to explain about their hair. One high school girl, who had been forced to leave school because she had permed hair just twelve days before her graduation, sued the high school and the principal. But the judge approved the school rule and she lost the suit.

Japanese students are closely controlled by school rules. Here are other examples:

Hairstyle. One third of middle school boys are required to have a closely clipped hair style. Others are prohibited to have hair long enough to reach the eyes, ears or neck. For girls, short hair is preferred, and not in a special cut. Long hair must be bound with a black rubber band. Ribbons and accessories are prohibited.

Uniforms. Standard school uniforms are black jacket with a closed collar for boys and navy blue sailor collar dresses for girls. There are strict rules for the length of the skirt, the width of the trousers, and the length of the jacket. Some schools require uniforms not only at school but whenever pupils go out from home out of school hours.

Belongings. School bags, shoes, overcoats, and belts are sometimes required to be certain colors, shapes and sizes. In some schools, even the color of underwear is part of the uniform, and teachers will check it!

Outside school life. School rules require a curfew, and clothing codes, and restrict access to certain places. Bowling alleys and video game arcades are off limits. Only movies which have been approved by schools may be seen with a parent or in the company of more than three other people.

Some schools have more than one hundred school rules like the ones listed. It is difficult to be creative and independent after being molded into a type while young.

Japanese men tend to wear the same dark suits and ladies the same fashion in dresses with the same hairstyle even after they are grown up, because of not wanting to be the nail that sticks out.

Chapter Fourteen

Manuals

The Japanese are always afraid of doing something different from others. This is why people depend on manuals for many occasions. If you do go into any book store in Japan – and if you can read Japanese – you will find numerous kinds of manuals on how to act when invited to weddings or funerals, how to answer questions at job interviews, and even how to date and how to confess your love to you lover, and so on.

These manuals explain details such as what you wear, what kinds of gifts to give, appropriate cash gifts, how to call, what to say, how to write, and what to do.

People follow what manuals say so that they will not make mistakes. Not only ceremonial occasions, but almost every meeting by governments, municipalities, businesses and even academic bodies have written scenarios for meeting procedures.

Here is an example. This is part of a scenario for a committee organized by a city council:

Official: We would like to begin the meeting. Thank you very much for your attendance today. You may have a handout of the agenda. Now we commence with the proceedings. First, we will have an

	election for the new chairman. According to the guidelines, we elect the chairman by mutual vote.
Committee Member:	I have a proposal. I recommend Mr. X as next chairman.
Official:	Now we have a proposal from Mr. A for Mr. X as chairman. Are there any objections? [No objections.]
Official:	We accept the proposal. Mr. X, you are elected as chairman. Please come to the seat for the chairman and give us an acceptance speech.
Chairman	[speech]
Official:	Thank you Chairman; please conduct the meeting.

Thus, the meeting proceeds by following the written scenario to the end. In this case, the official in charge has already negotiated with all the committee members and has had consent concerning the new chairman. Even though it had been called an election, the new chairman had been elected before the meeting started. That is why the scenario can say 'no objections.'

Job-hunting is a serious matter for college seniors, who follow the manuals on how to get a job. The manuals teach them how to apply, how to write a résumé, what to wear for job interviews, how to answer and how to behave at interviews. In Tokyo, especially in springtime, you may recognize them easily because they all have the same kind of suit, the same hairstyle and the same file holder, as the manuals instruct. In department stores you can find counters marked 'recruit wear' selling suits for job-hunters.

University professors often recommend to follow up someone else's research when students ask for the subject of their theses. If a student wants to do something very creative, the professor may advise not to take a risk and force a change of plan.

When the Kobe earthquake occurred, Prime Minister Murayama was accused of delaying in sending the rescue operation. He answered at the congress that he delayed because he did not know what to do, as there was no precedent for this situation. Even for saving someone's life, manuals are needed.

Chapter Fifteen
The Public Eye

In Japan, when children do something wrong or bad, their parents scold them by saying, 'If you do that, people will laugh at you.' Children are not made aware of what was bad in their action, but simply that they have stepped beyond the boundaries acceptable to their society. It is important for a person not to be made a laughing stock, or to be embarrassed in front of other people. Therefore, the same action, if done when no one was looking, may not have been considered wrong.

In Judeo-Christian society, the relationship between God and the individual ultimately determines good and evil. Therefore, evil is evil whether another person is there to witness it or not. However, in Japan, the relationship is between society and the individual. One must try not to bring shame upon oneself in the society in which one lives. One must always be aware of one's place in society.

The Japanese feel commonly embarrassed when:
One fails in front of others;
One is laughed at in front of others;
One cannot do what others do;
One's secrets are divulged;
One is honored or praised in front of others;
One is dressed differently from others.

As illustrated by the list above, any time when you find yourself standing alone away from the rest of society, you feel shameful or embarrassed.

On the other hand, the Japanese have a notion that, 'If everyone else is doing it, then I can do it too.' There is a popular saying, 'There's a red light, but if we all cross together, we don't need to be afraid.' I think this clearly illustrates the group consciousness of Japanese society. People know that they have to stop at the red light, yet, they don't care if everybody does.

There is a phobia called *taijinkyofusho*. This is to be afraid of other people. To be constantly afraid of what people are thinking about you is a result of the Japanese society requiring you always to be aware of how your actions look to others.

In surveys asking, 'Do you care about the differences you have with other people?', the age groups responded 'yes' as follows:

twenties:	79.5%
thirties:	81%
forties:	91%
fifties:	88.1%
sixties:	96.9

Listed below is a further breakdown of thoughts and actions:

	Yes	No
I live differently from the average Japanese	12%	84%
It is boring to have similar lifestyles	25%	71%
I use fashion to express myself	18%	78%
I like to be the center of attention	20%	77%

Looking at the results, it can be seen that most of the Japanese are looking to fit into the group. One does not want to be embarrassed by not belonging to society.

As can be seen, the foundation of Japanese moral philosophy lies not in God, but in society. Therefore, one must always balance one's own needs against those of society, so as not to be an outcast.

Chapter Sixteen

Silence and Smile

Many teachers and professors who teach Japanese students must be frustrated with their silence. Hosts and hostesses who invite Japanese guests to dinner parties struggle to make conversation while their Japanese guests just sit smiling quietly. For Westerners, silence in social settings often gives a negative impression.

If students are quiet in a classroom, the teacher worries that they have not understood, or are slow. If the guests are quiet at the dinner table, the host may be concerned that they are not interested in the topic or that they are bored or uncomfortable. For the Japanese, on the other hand, silence is very comfortable. Silence gives a positive impression in most cases in Japanese society. Quiet people are regarded as deeper thinkers than talkative people.

In Japanese classrooms, quiet students are always regarded as good students. They answer questions asked by the teacher, but it is rare for students to raise questions to the teacher: it is rude to ask something of the teacher in Japanese classrooms. Even when the teacher asks if they have questions, students are usually quiet. There are no courses such as 'debate' or 'oratory' in Japanese schools, so the Japanese students are not trained in public speaking. Even at academic meetings, scholars do not raise questions to the speakers, and question and answer sessions are not usually held after lectures.

Traditionally Japanese families never speak while eating meals. It is regarded as bad manners. Until recently, if children started to talk, fathers would scold them and tell them not to talk until they had finished their meal. These days, this tradition seems to be fading away in many families, yet many Japanese families watch television programs while they eat, so they do not talk anyway.

The Japanese reckon to understand each other without talking. The 'no talk, just work' type is the most praised in Japanese society. If there are several Japanese people together and their rankings are different, lower-ranking people are usually quiet in front of higher-ranking people.

Japanese people rarely talk or smile to strangers, and are surprised when Americans smile when they are just passing by on the street.

The so-called 'Japanese smile' makes people think we are inscrutable, because Japanese people smile in so many different situations. We smile when we feel happy, sad, angry, embarrassed, or even when we do not know an answer. Teachers will be puzzled with a Japanese student who just smiles and does not speak when asked a question. Often the smile means that someone doesn't know the answer and feels sorry or embarrassed.

Sometimes a Japanese person will tell you his or her problem or sad news with a smile. This smile means, 'I have told you about my private life; it is really nothing to worry about, so please do not worry.' It is, in a way, an apology for telling a story that will cause worry for other people.

We may smile when we want to cry. That means we try to hide our feelings behind the smile. The Confucian background teaches not to express feelings openly; rather, even when one is sad, one is taught at smile at others.

Lafcadio Hearn (1850–1904), an Irish-Greek writer who emigrated to Japan in 1890, explained the Japanese smile as one example of traditional courtesy and silent language. The Japanese smile is a way of communicating and establishing ties with a companion, and is a sign of assimilation. (Hearn's volumes dealing with Japan include the well-known *Japan: An Attempt at Interpretation*. He adopted the Japanese name Koizumi Yakumo.)

Even when one is sad, one is taught to smile to others. Therefore, it would be hasty to conclude that Japanese people are unemotional, unfeeling, or disinterested.

Chapter Seventeen

Gift Giving

Some of you have may experienced receiving gifts from Japanese people with no reasons you can think of, and wondered why they gave you such a precious gift. Or you might have witnessed Japanese tourists spending hundreds of dollars to buy souvenirs, sometimes dozens, of the same items. For the Japanese, gift giving is a form of non-verbal communication to maintain smooth relationships.

For many Japanese tourists, travel abroad is like a shopping trip. Many rush to designer stores and duty-free shops, sometimes paying no attention to actually touring. Information networks are now so well developed that Japanese tourists know exactly where to eat, sleep, and shop around the world. Guidebooks even list the prices of suggested goods. Most Japanese people travel with their trusted guidebook in one hand and a shopping list in the other hand. One may wonder if there is any fun involved in this kind of travel.

So what causes this shopping frenzy? Looking back in history, the word *omiyage* or 'gifts' comes originally from the souvenirs sold at the temples and shrines. In the past, travel meant a pilgrimage to temples and shrines made by representatives of a village. Before their departure, the whole village would gather to celebrate and give money and charms. In return, the representatives would bring back simple souvenirs from the temple or shrine for the villagers. This tradition is carried on to this day. Many travelers leave with money and charms given to them by relatives and friends. Then, during the trip, the traveler must purchase gifts to bring back to these people.

The Japanese are fond of gifts, and not just on occasions related to travel. For example, it is not polite to visit a person empty-handed. One usually brings sweets or other seasonal treats.

There are many other occasions when people give money or gifts, *ochugen*, a mid-year gift in July, and *oseibo*, a year-end gift in December, are typical of these occasions. Around July and December, one floor of every department store is transformed into an area only selling boxed gifts. Crowds of people gather around boxes and baskets here to compare prices. When a selection is made, the customer pays and writes down the destination and the name of the recipient. The package is then delivered directly from the store to the recipient. These gifts are sent to relatives, bosses, and other people involved in everyday life. Each gift is usually worth 1–2% of the giver's monthly salary, so the money spent can amount to quite a lot depending on the number of people to whom one must send these gifts. Around this time of year, many companies give bonus money which goes toward purchasing these gifts.

The gift boxes generally contain food, spice, liquor, towels, sheets, or basic everyday items. It is also traditional for employees to give and employers to receive. Therefore, the younger workers with the least money will not receive gifts, but must give gifts with their future promotions in mind. The receivers take note of the people who have sent the gifts, but do not particularly care about the gifts themselves. If they do not need any items, sometimes the gifts are rewrapped and given to another person. The gifts are not tailored to a particular person but are interchangeable.

Politicians, bureaucrats, professors, teachers, and lawyers all receive these gifts from voters, business-related people, students and clients. In Japanese society, most people do not realize some of these gifts are forms of bribery.

The Ministry of Education appreciates the tradition of gift giving as well. From 1987, the Ministries of Education, Foreign Affairs and the Interior established JET (The Japan Exchange and Teaching Program). The JET program, among other things, recruits young English-speaking graduates to teach English in Japanese high schools and junior high schools. For those young adults who are chosen for the program, the Ministry issues a general guidebook about life in Japan. In the chapter on gifts it is written that:

> Gift giving is an important part of Japanese culture. Non-Japanese people may not feet obliged to obey the custom, but a gift may indicate affection, appreciation, or respect. The Japanese, on the other hand, think it is an obligation.

The guidebook goes on to suggest bringing some kind of gifts to the people you will work with in Japan. Suggested gifts are famous-brand whiskeys or spirits, ceramics, coasters, calendars, teatowels, bookmarks, china thimbles, any souvenir particular to your country, area, or home-town, or anything with a recognized brand name (e.g. Burberry from England). The guidebook concludes by saying, 'Anything is well received. But don't go overboard – many people end up drinking their spare whiskey! Remember, if you are stuck you can always buy cakes, biscuits and chocolates in Japan.' (1987 edition)

The young adults on the JET program would be in-debted to teachers and bureaucrats. Therefore, the Japanese

Ministry of Education is encouraging the giving of whiskey to Japanese educators by American youngsters. Many Japanese people recognize that this is a bad custom, but if others are doing it they must also do it. Besides these seasonal gifts mentioned, there are gifts for weddings, births, entrances into schools, funerals, and many other occasions. On each occasion, one must think of gifts according to one's standing in society.

In Western culture, gifts are meant to be things tailored to particular people, perhaps even handmade. However, in Japan, handmade goods are not proper. Gifts wrapped in paper from famous department stores are much more appreciated. People are much more concerned with the price of the gift than its content. The person receiving the gift is able to measure the loyalty of the giver by how much was spent, not by the gift.

On average, gifts are exchanged twenty-three times per household, per year. The total amount spent on gifts alone averaged the equivalent of about two thousand US dollars in 1990.

Movements are being made toward abolishing some of this formal gift giving. However, these movements have never been successful because the Japanese communicate their feelings and measure the depth of relationships by means of objects.

Chapter Eighteen

Suicide

Suicide happens all around the world. Japan, contrary to popular belief, does not have the larger number of cases compared to other parts of the globe. According to the World Health Organization, Japan is eleventh after Hungary, Denmark, Austria, Switzerland, Finland, Czechoslovakia, West Germany, Belgium, Sweden and France. However, Japanese words such as *harakiri* and *kamikaze* have been internationalized and are now found in dictionaries around the world.

Though suicide involves an individual ending his own life, this private act is often influenced by society and culture. Among the many forms of suicide, there is multiple suicide which in Japan includes family suicide.

Family suicide may follow the social disgrace of a family member. For example, if a husband is involved in a scandal, the whole family may commit suicide. There are many cases in which the wife, devastated by her husband's extramarital affair and his or her disregard for family manners, commits suicide and kills the children. According to statistics, ninety percent of family suicide is this mother-child suicide where the mother is between the ages of twenty-five and thirty-five and the child is under the age of four. Of course, young children do not choose to die themselves and therefore are killed by the mother. Even now, a child under the age of thirteen is killed every day by a parent as a part of family suicide.

These killings occur because a Japanese mother, blinded by her love for the child, does not see the child as an individual, but as part of her. The child is killed without consent and, even though the mother generally kills the child, the blame is placed on the husband who forced this kind of situation while sympathy gathers for the mother.

Although it is not practiced nowadays, *harakiri* is a uniquely Japanese way of committing suicide. Traditionally, a short knife is held in the right hand and then stabbed under the left rib cage and pulled quickly across to the right. If there is an attendant standing behind the person, then it is at this time that the neck is cut from behind. If not, the short knife is pulled out and the person committing *harakiri* stabs it into his own heart or throat. The human stomach is the worst place for a lethal cut because of all the muscle and fat that surrounds it. According to old documents, the earliest death takes six hours, and in some cases over seventy-two hours.

Why cut the stomach? In Japan, it is believed that the soul is in the stomach. In Japanese, 'a person with a dark stomach' means a person doing evil deeds; 'a person with a big stomach' means a person who tolerates; 'to upset the stomach' means to be angry; 'to harden the stomach' means to be determined. It can be clearly seen that 'stomach' is used to embody various thoughts and characteristics, much the way 'heart' is used in Western cultures. Therefore, *harakiri*, which means 'to cut the stomach', is to prove one's courage by taking out the soul. In other words, it is a silent method of self-expression.

When does one commit *harakiri*? When one takes responsibility for mistakes. During the civil war era, the lord would die to defend his honor in defeat. Sometimes, people close to the master would also commit *harakiri* to be together with him. At other times, *harakiri* was not the choice of the individual, but the punishment for a crime.

In the Meiji era, the warrior society was dismantled, swords were taken away, and *harakiri* as a form of punishment was also stopped. However, *harakiri* used as a method of suicide did not subside. In 1912, when the era ended with the death of the emperor, his right hand man, Maresuke Nogi, dressed up for his funeral, read a traditional death poem, left a letter, and, with the temple bells ringing to bring in the new year, committed *harakiri*. His wife, after making sure her husband was dead, stabbed herself in the heart with the short knife.

After this incident, *harakiri* slowly faded, and the world was astonished when Yukio Mishima committed the act. Mishima (1925–1970) was the best known Japanese writer in the Western world. A flamboyant figure in life, he has become a legend since his suicide, which followed an unsuccessful attempt to foment rebellion among the ranks of his country's Self Defense Force.

Harakiri, unlike hanging or jumping suicide, is embedded in Japanese culture; it shows determination, strength, courage and can look admirable.

When a major political scandal is exposed, one or two loyal henchmen, though not ringleaders, may commit suicide to silence themselves and to show loyalty to their leaders. Although the way of committing suicide is different from *harakiri*, today's Japanese still see the spirit of *harakiri* in this demonstration of loyalty.

In the case of the baseball commissioner mentioned at the beginning of the book, he probably wanted to show his loyalty both to the American baseball player and his team through his death.

Chapter Nineteen
Belief

1. Statistics

I always have trouble answering the question raised by Westerners about the Japanese sense of religion. Do you think the Japanese are religious? If so, what kind of religion do we subscribe to? Of course, Buddhism, right? Or Shintoism?

Certainly, there are Buddhist temples and Shinto shrines everywhere in Japan, both in the rural villages and in the big cities. They are always clean and have many offerings. People stop by temples and shrines, give a short prayer and throw some money into the offertory boxes.

If you visit Japan on New Year's Day and observe crowds at the temples and shrines, you would believe without any doubt that the Japanese are very religious people. Indeed, eighty-two million people – three quarters of the total population – visit temples and shrines every New Year's Day and pray for happiness in the coming year.

However, if you ask Japanese people what kind of religion they believe in, they may answer with embarrassment, without self-confidence, and in a very soft voice, 'Buddhism'. And if you ask what Buddhism is, they will not answer, or honestly say, 'I don't know.' What does it mean that they don't know about the religion in which they believe? You may worry about them but in fact, this is

typical of the Japanese. There is a poem composed by
Saigyo (1118–1190), a famous poet of the Heian period:
'Even I do not know what kind god is in the shrine; I feel a
holy spirit and drop tears.' These are just the right words to
express Japanese religious sentiment. It doesn't matter if
you are in a Buddhist temple, a Shinto shrine, or even a
Christian church; if you feel something divine, you bow
your head and feel the blessings.

Here are statistics published by the Japanese Agency of
Cultural Affairs showing the numbers of followers of the
various religions in Japan:

Shintoist	106,643,616 (83% of the total population)
Buddhist	95,765,996 (79% of the total population)
Christian	1,486,588 (1% of the total population)
Others	10,833,994 (8% of the total population)

Agency of Cultural Affairs, 1993

The total number of followers of the Japanese religions is
over two hundred million, or close to twice the population!

However, according to a public opinion poll by a
Japanese newspaper, 28% of people are religious and 69%
of the people believe nothing. As for the younger
generation (under thirty years of age), only 8% believe in a
specific religion while 90% believe in none.

What do these contradictions mean? These are my
interpretations.

Shinto shrines are everywhere in Japan. In the town
where I grew up, there was a small shrine where a festival
was held once a month. I always looked forward to the
festival, where I could enjoy myself eating cotton candy
and playing all kinds of games. In the summertime, a
festival was held that lasted for several days. Young men
carried portable shrines through the streets amid a tumult,

while children pulled a festival car. In the evening – everybody – women and men, young and old – enjoyed 'Bon dance' with the loud sound of drums. The festival is still one of the biggest events in the summer for the Japanese.

For this festival, the Shinto shrine asks the parishioners for donations. Each household near the shrine donates some amount according to their income. Because the households located near the shrine are regarded as the parish, and each of the members in the households is counted as constituting Shinto followers. Therefore, the number of members in the parish of 88,000 Shinto shrines all over Japan is almost the same as the total population.

Many Japanese households have a family tomb at a Buddhist temple. There is a family name on each grave-stone, and after the death of a family member, the individual's name is carved on the back side of the grave-stone and the ashes are put underneath. Many people visit their family grave several times a year to wash the stone, place flowers on it, and burn incense. Some people even talk to the grave and offer food and *sake* (Japanese wine). All households that maintain a family tomb at a Buddhist temple are regarded as believers in Buddhism. This is why the number of 'Buddhists' is so high.

The number of Christians, 1% of the population, is quite accurate. This is because Christians profess their faith without any connection with community or ancestor. The number of Christians hasn't changed for one hundred years, in spite of the tremendous efforts of foreign missionaries as well as the Japanese clergy.

If I were to live in Japan, I would automatically become a member of the parish of the Shinto shrine nearest my home, as well as a member of the Buddhist temple where my ancestors are buried. Since I am already Christian, I would be counted as a follower of Shintoism, Buddhism and Christianity.

What about the public opinion poll? It showed that 69% of the population professes no religion. But 38% among those non-believers answered 'yes' to the question, 'Do you think religion is important for humankind?' What does this mean? I think those non-believers have never learned a particular religion or professed faith, yet they think it is good to have religious foundations. Therefore, it would be wrong to determine that 69% of the people are atheists who are strongly against religion. Although saying they are non-believers, they may still visit a shrine on New Year's Day and pray for happiness through the year, get married in a Christian church, swearing love to each other forever in the name of God, or have a funeral service at the Buddhist temple.

The contradiction between those statistics published by the Agency of Cultural Affairs and the public opinion poll show different definitions of 'religion'. That is to say, visiting shrines and temples are religious actions in a broad sense, yet not necessarily done as acts of faith. Sometimes people do not even know what kind of god the shrine they are visiting is dedicated to. It would be the equivalent of Westerners who go to church only at Christmas or Easter time just to enjoy the feeling of the season. Many Japanese also visit graves and attend Buddhist services as a custom but not as an act of faith. Many people declare themselves to be non-believers even though they visit shrines and temples quite often, because they have never studied the religion and never professed their faith. For this reason, it is not valid to determine that the Japanese are either religious or atheists only by looking at the statistics.

2.   Diversity of Belief

Only 19% of the Japanese answered 'Yes, it is strange,' to the question, 'Do you think it strange that a person believes in several religions at once, like Shintoism and Buddhism?' 77% answered, 'No, it is not strange. It is normal.' It is especially worth noting that only 40% of the Christians were against it. 60% of the Christians who professed a belief in one God said, 'It's not strange. It is okay.' You may understand from these answers how difficult it is to root Christianity on Japanese soil.

The house where I grew up had a small shrine in the living room attached to a wall near the ceiling. This was supposed to protect the house and family according to the Shinto belief. Since my grandparents were buried at the family tomb at a Buddhist temple, there was also a family altar, with the memorial tablet of my grandparents on it, in the living room near the small shrine.

My parents, who became Christian after they married, never got rid of the small shrine and family altar. They even continue to worship them. On the memorial day of our grandparents, we often went to the Buddhist temple and listened to a religious chants performed by the Buddhist priest. And yet my parents were devout Christians who served as a board member of the church council and taught Sunday school for many years.

This is not true for just my parents. This is quite normal for many Japanese people. Even a Buddhist priest may send his daughter to a Christian missionary school because these provide a better education. A kindergarten attached to a Shinto shrine may celebrate Christmas because the children love Santa Claus. This is a typical way to act. When young couples are getting married, religious beliefs are a low priority. The bride and groom don't care what religion the other follows. Religion does not have a powerful influence on the important decisions of the Japanese.

3. Prayer for Profit

It is not an exaggeration to say that the reason many Japanese people visit temples and shrines is to ask for profit in this world. In the season of school entrance examinations, shrines and temples are covered with *emas*, small wooden votive tablets with wishes written on them. Students and their families visit shrines and temples to pray for success in their exams, and write their wishes on the *ema* to hang around the temples.

Incense is also burnt, usually in front of the temples. People will come to apply the smoke to their bodies, heads, eyes, feet, or whenever they have problems, since it is believed that it will heal them and solve their problems.

There are many modern buildings in the big cities of Japan, but sometimes you will see small traditional shrines on the roofs. The world-famous workaholic Japanese businessmen worship these shrines and pray for the prosperity of their companies.

In this way, the Japanese people pray for the safety, happiness and prosperity of individuals, societies and nations.

4. Ancestor Worship

According to a public opinion poll, 74% of the Japanese visit the family tomb once or twice a year. However, these actions are not observed from faith, but rather from custom. Visiting the family tomb, or ancestor worship, is a significant factor in family religion. If a family member dies, a funeral service is usually held according to the Buddhist ritual, and a memorial service is held regularly, going by the Buddhist calendar, until fifty years after death.

After that time, it is believed that the spirit loses its individuality.

Even Japanese Christians wish to have this type of memorial service for their families, so some Japanese Christian churches hold a memorial service on All Saints Day or at Easter to honor these ancestors. This is one good example of the 'Japanization' of Christianity.

When people are killed in an airplane crash or a maritime accident, the bereaved family will often visit the spot where the accident occurred. If it happened in the ocean, they will visit the spot by boat and throw flowers or pour *sake*, which the deceased may have liked, to comfort the spirit. In 1987, there was a terrible crash deep in the mountains in the central part of Japan. Almost all those aboard the plane were killed instantly. Even though it was in an untrodden high mountain region, many of the bereaved wished to visit the spot and some of them did. Today, there is a road to the site and a monument to those who died there. Every year, many bereaved relatives climb the mountain on the anniversary of the accident. For those who cannot go to the top of the mountain, a small *jizo*, or guardian deity of the people, was built halfway up the mountain. People believe that they can meet the spirits of the accident victims at that spot. They also have a grave at the temple graveyard in the home town, as well as a family altar with a memorial tablet in their own home. The family members worship at this altar in the morning and evening. The spirits of the dead must be quite busy moving from place to place so their relatives can pray for them!

People hold memorial services not only for human beings, but also for animals, dolls, and even for needles. This is also true in universities or laboratories where animals and other living things are used for experiments; memorial services are held for these animals on a regular basis. Some establishments even build monuments to them. The order of a memorial service for animals held by a university laboratory lists all the kinds and numbers of the living things which were used for experiments during the year. The service is led by a Shinto priest, and, as a result, professors and students believe that the spirits of the rats, tadpoles, colitis germs and so on which were sacrificed for science research may rest in peace.

People believe that dolls have souls too. When dolls get old and no longer have any use, people bring them to the temple on the day of the memorial service for dolls, and burn them with a holy fire giving thanks for them. People even believe that needles have souls. On the day of the memorial service for needles, people bring their needles to the temple and pierce them into soft *tofu* giving thanks for their hard work. At the same time, they pray for the improvement of their sewing skills.

For the spirits of unborn children, who could not begin their lives in this world due to miscarriage or abortion, people build a *mizuko jizo* or a guardian deity of the child. With this, they pray for peace in those spirits. Nowadays, many women who have had abortions visit temples and have their own *jizo* built to ask for salvation from their sins.

5. Superstition

On the Japanese calendar, you will find strange Kanji or Chinese characters under the date. They are *sensho*, *tomobiki*, *senpu*, *butsumetsu*, *taian*, and *shakko*. These six words tell you the fortune of the day. For example, *taian* means a day of good fortune, and people are pleased to have a wedding ceremony or other happy occasion on that day. On these days, many wedding centers and hotels are fully booked, conducting ceremonies every half hour. However, on a day of bad fortune like *butsumetsu* (the day of Buddha's death), nobody would dare have a wedding ceremony, and they will often close their business for the day. On the day of *tomobiki* ('bring over your friend'), people are willing to have weddings but funerals must be avoided; on that day, crematoriums are closed. In this way, everyday life for almost all Japanese people are affected by the cycle of the six words on the calendar. Statistics show that 76% of the Japanese population follow this calendar.

The Chinese Zodiac calendar also has a big influence on the Japanese people. Twelve animals – rat, cow, tiger, rabbit, dragon, snake, horse, sheep, monkey, rooster, dog and boar – were traditionally used to tell the direction, the hour, and the day as well as the year. Today it is mainly used to categorize the year. For instance, I was born in 1945, the year of the rooster. In addition, people believe that their personalities are similar to the animal of the year of their birth. You may hear people say such things as, 'Now I understand why you are so gentle, because you were born in the year of the sheep', or, 'He is so rough because he was born in the year of the tiger'. My mother often used to say to me, 'You are careless because you were born in the year of the rooster!'

Matchmakers consider their candidates' animal year very seriously when they make matches.

There is a superstition in Japan that women who are born in the year called *hinoeuma*, which occurs every sixty years, are very strong and may kill their husbands. Because of this, people are afraid to have a baby in that year. The most recent *hinoeuma* was 1966. If you look at Japanese population statistics, you will see a lower birth rate in 1966. This is a result of people controlling themselves, trying not to have a baby in that year because they didn't want a baby girl born in *hinoeuma*. A Japanese newspaper once printed a young women's letter saying, 'I almost married a nice man, but when he found out I was born in the year of *hinoeuma*, his mother forced him to cancel our engagement.' This superstition is still strongly believed among ordinary Japanese people.

Many people also believe in lucky and unlucky directions and orientations. When people build a house, they avoid having doors face to *kimon* the (Devil's gate) to the north-east. They will also avoid traveling in an unlucky direction, or will make detours to avoid the unlucky direction. For example, suppose your destination is south and a fortune-teller tells you that that is a bad direction: you would avoid going straight south, but, for example, go east first. From that point your destination would be located south-west and would be safe. The Japanese do not sleep with pillows facing north, because only the dead lay their heads to the north.

You will see all sorts of fortune-tellers on the streets of the big cities in Japan, and many young women forming lines to wait their turn. Today, palm readers have computerized and do a good business.

Many people keep good luck amulets, and many cars will display these in the car windshield.

In this way, these superstitious customs have become a part of Japanese life. The origin of these customs is mainly Confucianism, Taoism, or Inyodo. In this sense at least, religious influence is great among the Japanese.

Chapter Twenty

Family

1. Married Couples

After a man and a woman get married in Japan, they often give up living as individuals, preferring to become as one unit. The spouse is like the air we breathe. It's not something we constantly see and feel the presence of, yet we cannot live without it. Because they are at one and are so relaxed with each other, they no longer pay attention to their looks. The wife will stop putting on make-up for her husband. The husband does not care how he looks to his wife, and will take off his jacket and shirt once he comes home, or even his trousers and socks in the summer. He may feel quite relaxed wearing only his underwear in the living room.

In public, a couple expresses one opinion. Even if they have different opinions, which may be discussed privately between the two of them, when others are around, the wife agrees with her husband. Of course, because they are one body, they do not need to confirm their love by saying, 'I love you' every day.

The husband may introduce his wife by saying, 'This is my silly wife', while the wife smiles. They understand each other deeply; the wife knows that her husband does not think she is silly at all. She understands that he expresses his humbleness by mentioning his better half instead of himself. A wife, in turn, would not speak of her husband as a capable man, because this would be bragging about herself.

In the West, the husband and wife have individual identities which they fear losing in marriage. But in Japanese culture, couples give up presenting themselves as individuals after they marry. In Western culture, John and Mary are the same John and Mary even after they are married. In Japanese tradition, once John and Mary are married, they become the Smiths. Their individuality as John and Mary is nil.

In Japan, a wife signing her husband's name or putting her husband's seal on a document is an everyday occurrence. In Japan, a signature does not have any binding power. Instead, a stamp or seal, which you can buy at any stationery shop or train station kiosk for the equivalent of five or six dollars, has legal power. This *hanko*, or seal, is a necessity in Japanese daily life. One needs it to withdraw money from a bank account, to receive a parcel from a mailman, to change one's address, to apply for a job, to submit documents to a school, and so on. With her husband's seal, a wife can substitute for her husband and deal with almost everything; therefore it is very common among Japanese couples for the wife to sign her husband's name, and not her own name, on any document which needs certification.

2. Man's World, Woman's World

Westerners may have the impression that in Japan, dominance of men over women forces women to lead a miserable life. This is a misconception.

In a typical modern Japanese white-collar worker's family, husband and wife usually divide the work. That is, the husband works outside for a living, and the wife works at home doing the housework and raising children. The husband gives all of his pay to his wife and receives his daily spending money. The wife holds the purse strings, does the daily shopping, and takes care of the children and their education.

The husband and wife never invade each others' territory, and instead trust and depend on each other. Therefore, a wife does not show interest in her husband's work, and pays little attention to what he is doing. A husband trusts his wife to handle the family finances and bring up the children.

Because they are one body, husband and wife believe that they can understand each other without talking. Often, keeping to their own territory, they speak very little to each other.

After the husband comes home from work, he sometimes asks his wife to help him change his clothes, eats a fully prepared meal, and goes to sleep on a futon which has been prepared by his wife.

It may look as if the wife is serving her husband like a slave, but as a matter of fact, she is the one who has power in the family.

A husband may have a lot of acquaintances from work, yet his wife may hardly know them. Wives have friends through neighbors and children's schools and the husband is often not interested in them. Husbands and wives rarely introduce their friends to their spouses. Whenever I return to Japan, I try to meet with my friends. We women often have a good time eating and chattering until late at night. My husband also meets his friends, who are only men, at a bar and they drink and talk until late, too, so, even though we go back to Japan together, strange to say, we have few chances to see friends together.

3. 'Witty Wife'

Though many Japanese husbands and wives lead their lives dividing their work, it does not mean that they don't cooperate with each other. When the wife helps her husband feign ignorance, this is called *naijo no koh* or 'witty wife'. These wives are regarded as the ideal. The ideal wife is usually modest and reticent toward her husband, yet watches him carefully so that when he needs help she can instantly help him without injuring his honor.

The stories of, 'The Wife of *Yamanouchi Kazutoyo*' and, 'The Wife of *Hanaoka Seishu*' are the most famous stories about *naijo no koh*. *Yamanouchi Kazutoyo* (1546–1605) was a poor samurai. When the news spread that the *Shogun Nobunaga* would visit their village to inspect samurais and their horses, the wife of *Kazutoyo* gave her dowry, which she had never mentioned before, to her husband and suggested that he buy a better horse. At the inspection, the *shogun* was very much impressed by *Kazutoyo*'s beautiful horse, and offered him a better position. *Kazutoyo* became a famous *Daimyo*, or feudal lord.

Hanaoka Seishu (1760–1835) was a medical doctor who learned Chinese and Dutch medicine in the Edo period. He is known as the first surgeon in the world to perform an operation using an anesthetic which was made from *datura*, or thorn apple. It was essential for him to have human guinea pigs to develop his research into anesthetics. Knowing this, his wife offered to become a subject for him. As a result, she lost her eyesight. She did not mind sacrificing herself if it meant success for her husband.

In Japanese culture, a witty wife is one who helps her husband without letting others know and without injuring her husband's honor.

4. *Kowa Kasugai*: Children are the Clamps which join Husband and Wife

After a married couple have children, their lifestyles become child-centered. The husband starts to call his wife 'mama' or 'mother', and the wife calls her husband 'papa' or 'father'. The mother may ask her son, 'Go get your father', but phrases such as, 'Mama, pick that up for me', or, 'Papa, why don't you take a bath now', can also be heard between husband and wife even when the children are not around.

In Japan, it is uncommon for a husband and wife to go out for dinner or a movie and leave the children at home with a babysitter. If they do, people will say that they are failures as parents. If they really need to go out without the children, they will usually ask one of their mothers or a close friend to take care of their children. Then they make sure they come home as soon as possible.

As the children grow, the conversation within the family becomes still more child-centered. Conversations between the husband and wife become fewer and fewer, and conversations between the mother and children or between the father and children become more common. If the parents want to go to a restaurant, the children almost always go. That's why there are many restaurants in Japan that cater for families.

There are many couples who wish to divorce in Japan. But in many cases they stay married only for the sake of their children. Children are indeed the clamps which join husband and wife.

5. Mother-Child Relationship

In a Japanese household you may find in a drawer a small wooden box with 'Longevity' printed in golden lettering on the top. My family had one in the house where I grew up in Tokyo, and I even have two of these boxes in my house in the US.

When my daughter found the box, she asked me, 'What is it?' I replied, 'It is a treasure,' and allowed her to open it. She could only find a small object wrapped in a piece of gauze. 'What is this?' she asked me again. I answered, 'This is your umbilical cord.' When she heard my reply, she threw it down, saying, 'How disgusting!'

I do not know exactly why the Japanese treat a small piece of dried umbilical cord as a family treasure, but they do and they keep it their whole lives. When I gave birth to my daughter in Japan, the doctor gave me a small, pretty box made of paulownia wood which contained the dried cord. I still have it. Since my son was born in a hospital in Switzerland, he does not have such a thing; his umbilical cord probably was thrown away by the nurse who was taking care of him. I don't know if there are any countries except Japan that treat an umbilical cord like an heirloom. It seems that this cord symbolizes the strong relationship between mother and child in Japan.

Since the famously 'workaholic' Japanese fathers work from early in the morning until late in the evening, often commuting very long distances, they may not get home until late at night. Even on weekends, they often need to go to business golf games, or other work-related engagements. The poor father often has no time to communicate with his family, especially with his children. Consequently, his wife has responsibility for raising the children alone, and the bond between the mother and the children is strengthened. While a child is a baby, the mother will always stay with it. When she needs to go out, she straps her baby on her back or takes the baby carriage and brings the baby wherever she needs to go.

Japanese mothers rarely think of spending time on their own hobbies or interests and leaving their children with babysitters. Thus, the relationship between such a devoted mother and such a protected child often continues even after the child grows up. In relation, the mother-son relationship is stronger than the mother-daughter one. Many young men say that they would not marry unless their mothers approved of the prospective bride. According to survey statistics, when the students of Tokyo university, the most prestigious university in Japan, are asked, 'Who do you most respect', the most common answer is, 'My mother'.

In one Japanese newspaper, there was a short letter from a mother. She wrote that after her son graduated from college and got a job, on the first payday he took her to a fine restaurant. She was very moved and proud of her son. That was all. There was nothing about her husband; it was not clear if he had died, if they were divorced or still married. Anyway, for this happy mother, she had completely forgotten about her husband and the son's father at that moment.

No one thinks twice in Japan when a well-dressed mother sits with her twenty-five-year-old son at a top restaurant and enjoys dinner without her husband.

6.   Father

Many Japanese fathers are often employed for life by the same company. Therefore, they have very loyal ties to their workplace, usually taking very few paid vacations. The average number of working hours for a Japanese worker is 2,150 hours per year, which is 500 hours longer than the average German worker and 200 hours longer than the average worker in the US.

Because they identify so strongly with their companies, men often say the name of their workplace with their own name when introducing themselves. One may say, 'I am, Sony's *Tanaka*', or, 'I am Mr. Kimura from the Ministry of Finance' and never even mention their professions, such as, 'I am an engineer', or, 'I am an accountant'.

Work often comes before family life. That's why only 18% of fathers can have dinner with their families on weekdays, though 90% of mothers hope that all the family members may get together at the dinner table.

Many a father will find that he is an outsider among his family when he is at home because he cannot follow the conversations between the mother and children.

In addition to this mental isolation, a man cannot find his own place, physically, in his own home. Because the housing situation is very bad in Japan, if a private room is given to the children, there is no room for the father except in the living room. In Japan, parents do not generally have their own bedrooms, and the living room is their bedroom at night. So, even if the father wants to go to sleep, if some other family member is watching TV or talking in the living room, he cannot spread out his *futon*.

If he cannot enjoy conversation with his family, and there is no room for him in his house, why should he go straight home after work? This is why many fathers stop at bars with their colleagues after work. Through chatting with colleagues, they may exchange important information. If his wife complains about his coming home late, a man explains that it is *nominucation*, a combination of two words, *nomu* (drink) and the English 'communication'. He will say it is an essential part of his job. If you take a late train, after 10 p.m., you will see it is packed with these fathers.

At the bar, the hostess is called 'mama' by the customers and she enjoys talking with these fathers. They chat with 'mama' about their stressful work or appalling colleagues while they are drinking. As she nods and listens attentively to them, they feel relaxed and eased from their hard work. It is even said that because of these 'mamas' very few psychiatrists are needed in Japan. It is very reasonable for the client if 'mama', takes the role of a counselor for the cost of a glass of wine, don't you think?

Japanese fathers once stood at the top of the family and family members had to obey whatever the father told them. But times have changed, and now the Japanese home is occupied by the mother and children, and the poor father only provides the salary. The recent watchword among wives is 'A good husband is healthy and not at home', which has swept away the traditional *naijo no ko* (wife's assistance).

7. Children

Most Japanese children, like their fathers, are workaholics. Though experts agree that children between the ages of ten and fifteen years old need eight and a half hours of sleep a night, over 30% of Japanese children sleep less than eight hours.

School hours are seven to eight hours a day, yet many children often study two more hours at *juku* (cramming school). *Juku* is a private, after-school class which concentrates mainly on techniques for earning high scores in entrance exams. Because Japanese schools have a half-day on Saturdays (with one Saturday a month off), with only forty days of summer vacation, children study 250 days a year in Japan. It is a very long school year compared to the 180 day school year in the US.

And even during the short summer vacation, children have a lot of homework and they attend *juku*.

The average playtime for elementary school children is 96 minutes each day. However, more than 20% of the children play for less than 30 minutes or take no time to play at all. (Over 40% of children play more than four hours a day in the US.)

Japanese mothers are happy to see their children studying, and try not to let them help in any housework. The most common words to be heard in a Japanese home are, 'Go study!' Japanese children generally help their mothers only 14 minutes a day.

The difference is great compared with the American children who help with the housework for 72 minutes a day. There are no jobs like baby-sitting in Japan, and only 2% of Japanese children have had the experience of a paid job.

Parents try to provide the best study conditions for their children, such as a private study room with air conditioning, a nice desk, a private TV and a stereo or CD system. Though receiving such treatment, only 34% of Japanese children show satisfaction with their lives. This is compared to 70% of foreign children who express satisfaction with their lives. Furthermore, Japanese children do not trust adults, and 74% percent of children express feelings that they don't want to be adults.

One of the reasons that children are not satisfied with their lives is because teachers grade their school work in a relative way (on a bell curve), not with an absolute grade. The relative grading means grading by proportions of each of the students. That means that 10% of the class get As, 20% of the students get Bs, 40% of the students get Cs, 20% get Ds and 10% get Es for each subject. For example, if you are in a class with forty students, only four can get As for each subject, even though more than four students may get over 90 points. Conversely, there should be four E-grade students, even though their points are not so bad. Therefore, classmates who get points close to each other become enemies and gloat if someone makes a mistake.

Many children express sadness that they cannot make real friends in school. Sad to say, that Japanese children are discontent with both school and social life while growing more materialistic and egotistical than ever.

8. College Students

Once those children who have studied so hard get into college, they stop studying. This is because the purpose of their studies was only to pass the entrance exams for college. In high school, students learn more about how to pass exams than they do about reading, research, or discussion. If you compare reading time after school with that of American or European children, Japanese children read less than half of that which Western children do. Why is it so important, then, to pass the college entrance exams? It is because, in Japanese society, the rank of a college is equal to the rank of a person's future job. Those students who graduate from more elite schools have the chance of a better job.

Since many big corporations and the government and municipal offices in Japan use a life employment and seniority system, once people are employed, their status is secured. Their salary rises according to the length of their service at the company, and most employees can stay until retirement age, usually fifty-five or sixty.

Once you pass the exams and become a college student, you can just enjoy four years at college, because you can graduate even if you cut classes. Compared with Western college professors, many Japanese professors are not so enthusiastic about teaching. There are no evaluations from the college or the students. Professors often cut classes, too, and repeat the same lectures every year, giving exams only once or twice a year. Thus, if professors repeat the same lectures every year and test students only once a year, it makes it quite possible to graduate without attending classes.

During college, many students enjoy their hobbies or earn money through part-time jobs instead of studying. Even though students lead such a lazy college life, 90% of parents believe it is their duty to pay tuition fees for their children.

9. The Twilight Years

When a couple starts to feel that they have completed the raising of their children, they are also reaching their retirement age. Since the husband will have been working at the same company for several decades, all of his relationships will have been company-related. When he retires from his work, he will realize that he has nothing left.

Because he had been working so hard, he does not know what he should do after he stops working. He feels that he has lost everything with his job. Usually he has few hobbies because he has had no time to enjoy them, nor does he have the curiosity to try new things. He is quite at a loss. Even the people who had been working under him pay no attention to him once he has left his position. The people who were acquainted with him through his work also leave him behind. He becomes shocked when he recognizes that he has no true friends who can share his joys and sorrows.

Even if he wants to talk more or travel with his wife, it is not an easy thing to do, for they have been living in such different worlds for such a long time.

For the wife, her husband's retirement will mean a big change in her life. This time is a highlight of her life as she has finished raising children and is having a good time with her friends. She would prefer to travel with her good friends than with her bored husband.

After the husband retires, he often stays home, and it becomes difficult for the wife to find her own time to spend with her friends because he often asks where she is going and demands that every meal be prepared on time.

Since she has only seen him briefly every day while he was working, a wife has not noticed the bad points of his personality; even if she has, she has been able to avoid them. But now if he stays home most of the time, she cannot stand it. The husbands who stay home with nothing to do are called *Sodai gomi* big trash or *nure ochiba* (wet falling leaves – it implies that they are hard to sweep away). Sometimes, this creates a problem between husband and wife.

There have been quite a few cases recently in which a wife demands she receive half of her husband's retirement in a lump sum, and wants a divorce. If she cannot divorce for some reason, she tries to avoid him and lives her own life even though they continue to live in the same house. It is called *kateinai rikon* (divorce in the house).

If parents divorce, the majority of children support their mothers, and the poor husband, who has never done housework before, does not know what to do.

10. The Elderly

Of course, there are many married couples who keep their marriages happily going until they have silver hair. But for many elderly people, the big issue is survival. The average life expectancy in Japan has reached seventy-six years for men and eighty-two years for women. In Japanese families for a long time, the relationships between the children and the parents were considered more important than the relationship between the wife and husband. This means that parents have an obligation to bring up their children and the children, have to support their parents when they get old. It is also important to keep up the family name and family job as well as the family graveyard. Until right before World War II, the parents could enjoy their retirement while living with the family of their first son, who was the legal heir to their property. However, since World War II, every value system in Japan has been changed drastically, including the sense of family support.

By 1960, almost 90% of the elderly had been living with the family of one of their children, not necessarily the first son any more. In the late 80s, 70% were still living with one of their children's families. If children let their old parents live alone, they are regarded as cold-hearted and are blamed by society.

In the cities, many young married couples leave their families and form their own nuclear families, yet they believe it is their duty to support their parents when they get old. The fact that people have felt the duty to support and live together with their parents has caused the Japanese government to neglect the elderly. The government's policy is to recommend that three generations live together, saying, 'It is beautiful to see the three generations surround a dinner table together.'

The level of personal savings in the average Japanese household is one of the highest in the world. Unfortunately, this money does not enable people to enjoy life after retirement. It only pays for unexpected accidents or hospitalizations after retirement, because there is not enough social security. To address this issue, the Ministry of International Trade and Industry (MITI) proposed the 'Silver Columbus Plan' in 1987. According to the this, the government would build communities for the elderly in low-cost countries such as Portugal, Spain, or Canada. How is it possible for old people who have never lived overseas or do not speak the language to live there? More-over, will these countries be willing to accept these elderly foreigners? This plan was criticized so heavily from both inside and outside Japan that it was abandoned.

Many big Japanese businesses reap huge profits because they invest their money in plant improvement and keep worker's salaries down. That is why people sometimes say, 'Rich Japan, Poor Japanese'. When the time comes that elderly people can enjoy that retirement with no worries about the future, Japan may truly be called a rich country.